Best Yorkshire Quotations

W.R. Mitchell

DALESMAN
1994

Dalesman Publishing Company
Stable Courtyard, Broughton Hall,
Skipton, North Yorkshire BD 23 3AE

First Published 1994
Copyright Dalesman Publishing

Compiled by **W.R. Mitchell**
Front cover by **T. Shaw**

A British Library Cataloguing in Publication
record is available for this book

ISBN 1 85568 080 7

Introduction

A Yorkshireman, like a dragoon, is nothing without his horse. So wrote Surtees, in one of his Jorrocks' stories. In contrast is the down-to-earth remark of a crusty Dalesman in the 1960s, that "farmers round here like wet weather. It keeps folks away."

This book contains a few of the many pithy remarks about people and places in Yorkshire - "the most renowned of shires" (Michael Drayton). The quotations are grouped together in subjects, presented alphabetically. This is a handbook for browsers, the inquisitive, the native-born who have a great pride in Yorkshire and the off-comers who want to know what that pride is all about.

Mark my words (as they used to say) Yorkshire is a great county. Thou'll 'appen hev 'eard (to use some of the native tongue) that before the disastrous local government re-organisation of 1974, Yorkshire had 3,906,940 acres - more acres, indeed, than there are words in the Bible.

I particularly like Daniel Defoe's observation on entering "the great county of York." He was "uncertain which way to begin to take a full view of it, for 'tis a county of a very great extent."

Some of the local customs, such as having Yorkshire "pudding" at the start of a meal, are apt to bemuse our visitors. A New Yorker who had eaten Yorkshire pudding half a dozen times remarked: "Each time, it's been a different shape, size and colour. I've had it with, without, under and above gravy, with and without meat. The whole thing is too mysterious."

The Yorkshire tongue, which so often sounds brusque to strangers, can be lyrical. Fred Lawson, the Wensleydale artist, who wrote as he spoke, noted (1967): "There was a little breeze, just enough to make the uncut grass and the trees move, and a sky the colour of opal. Tonight the smell of hay comes in at the door." Luvly!

We can stand any amount of criticism, as long as we're out of earshot. We don't mind perceptive comments. Graham Turner, in his book *The North Country*, referred to Hull as "an immensely parochial in-grown sort of town." And a resident of Helmsley left us a memorable quotation when describing Duncombe Park House, the former seat of the Fevershams, as "a near-miss Vanbrugh".

Yorkshire is a country in a county. In the west are the Pennines, Defoe's "hills of brass", with the Aire Gap separating the "striding dales" (Halliwell Sutcliffe) of the north from the industrialised valleys of the south.

In the north-east, across the fatty heartland of Yorkshire, lie tabular hills thatched with heather. The farms, villages and small market towns are roofed with red pantiles. The billowing wolds, once the haunt of sheep and rabbits, now comprise one of the most productive arable districts in England.

The North York Moors have a seaward termination in the soaring coastal cliffs, with Boulby, at over 600ft, as the highspot. The chalk which forms a crescent in the south-east has its sea-view as the white cliffs of Bempton and Flamborough.

That's just a beginning. Sir Rupert Hart-Davis (1967) rejoiced in changeless Swaledale, observing: "I used to have a cottage at Keld and the view from it must have been unchanged for two hundred years."

W.R. Lang, visiting Castleford in the 1960s, discovered that some aspects of an urban area had not changed. A kindly passer-by pointed "that way to t'town hall, owd luv!" Lang rejoiced, for "with that 'owd luv', the image snapped into focus. Castleford folk hadn't changed much, even if improvements to the town were immense, since the day I left it twenty years back..."

Let these quotations help us to Rejoice and Be Glad (to quote the Prayer Book) in our Yorkshire heritage.

W.R. MITCHELL

Dictionary

Abbeys

Practically the only thing that Yorkshire dales have in common is the fact that in every one you are almost certain to hit on a superb ruined abbey or castle.

S.P.B. Mais

Fountains Abbey held, by grant and lease, over a million acres of land in Craven and from them drew great stocks of wool.

Arthur Raistrick (1941)

We walked upon Mr Duncombe's terrace and looked down upon the Abbey (Rievaulx). It stands in a larger valley among a brotherhood of valleys, of different length and breadth - all woody, and running up into the hills in all directions.

Dorothy Wordsworth, The Grasmere Journal (1802)

Arncliffe

To me, this is a Midsummer Village. Under the bright sun, the sweet turf contrasts with bone-white limestone; and Cowside Beck, sparkling in its deep bed, contrasts with the Skirfare as viewed from the bridge. In summer, this stretch of the river is green, taking the hue of massed leaves.

W. R. Mitchell (1983)

Artists

More than anything else, it is the poets and painters of the Romantic era of the late eighteenth and early nineteenth centuries whose view of the countryside has dominated our own. In a very real sense, we see the Yorkshire Dales through their eyes.

Colin Speakman (1981)

Bolton Abbey has been made familiar for us by many painters since Landseer...A red-letter day for me, as a boy, was when I found Sir David

Murray, painting here, in waders; the long poles of his easel going down into the bed of the river, and screwed to the poles was a great and glowing canvas.

Ernest Forbes (1931)

There's nowhere quite like the Dales for painting.

Owen Bowen (1966)

Mr Bowen paints as spontaneously as a bird sings.

W. T. Oliver, art critic (1966)

Few painters can have made their reputation with less sensation than Reginald Grange Brundrit.

The Times obituary (1960)
about a man who had a studio at Grassington

When sanity returns to the visual arts, I think R. G. Brundrit will stand out as one of the greatest pure landscape painters of the present century.

Francis Wall

Barnsley

Thanks to Barnsley's human scale, no part of it is far from open country...Green rolling hills lead towards the high Pennines and grey stone villages have ancient churches.

Margaret Ottley (1978)

Batley

The walk to the town gives you such a view as can only be seen in a manufacturing district: hills, fields, meadows, and rough slopes, all bestrewn with cottages, factories, warehouses, sheds, clouded here and there by smoke; roads and paths wandering apparently anywhere; here and there a quarry, and piles of square stones; heaps of refuse; wheatfields among the houses; potato-plots in little levels, and everything giving you the impression of waiting to be finished.

Walter White (1861)

Beverley

...a place of skylines. There is hardly a part of the town from which, at any given moment, the vista of houses is not toppled by the silver-grey pinnacles of ecclesiastic art - the stately minster on the one hand, or the no less stately St Mary's church on the other.

S. J. B. (1935)

Beverley...its two great churches like some old ivory carving of the Japanese, rising from the russet medley of this old brick town.

Ernest Forbes

Bingley

It is a town tucked away in a pinched valley; a tight cluster of grey stone cottages and shops lying neatly between the Leeds-Liverpool Canal and the river Aire, with its modest red-brick suburbs spreading out along the road like a stain.

John Hewitt (1980)

Birds

The curlew is the symbol of the moors.

John Hillaby (1982)

Dippers...stocky, swift flying black birds with their brilliant white chests stand bobbing on every rock in those lovely pebbly streams and ghylls. Their covered mossy nests are clamped tight against sheer grey rocks, often overhanging a waterfall that sprays them as they sit.

F. H. Grisewood

When it's just brekkin' light, grouse start a-crowing to one another. And that's what we call t'quack.

Cowling man with free shooting rights on Ickornshaw Moor

I've tasted a few grouse, but I've never liked 'em. I wouldn't thank nobody for a grouse - not to eat.

Swaledale farmer

The golden plover is a strange, lonely bird with a solitary little call, *tee-oo-oo*.

John Hillaby (1982)

Bolton Abbey

The footman ran round the car and opened the rear door to reveal King George V in his tweed knickerbocker shooting suit and knee-length diamond patterned stockings... His brogues still had the previous day's mud on them. Fancy being King of England and having to wear dirty shoes!

Dorothy M. Dewhurst, in a party of Girl Guides, 1927

Bradford

This is a city bubbling with enthusiasm about itself. Its Victorian buildings sparkle in the sun; green swards replace the ugly derelict areas on the roads into the city centre and, wonder of wonders, it is marketing its appeal as an unusual tourist centre.

John Hewitt (1983)

Cheese

The monks (of Jervaulx, in Wensleydale) twice daily milked the ewes and introduced... a means of keeping the food value of surplus milk for winter use, when the fruits of the soils were scarce... Sheep have been superseded by the Shorthorn cow for the production of milk, but the process of manufacture of Wensleydale cheese has been handed down with slight alterations from mother to daughter since those Flemish holy men lived contentedly in the shadow of our hills.

T. C. Calvert (1939)

Cleveland

These lofty hills of Cleveland form a fitting background, with a character near akin to the mighty scarps and rugged steeps that are their buttresses against the sea.

John Leyland (1892)

Cleveland in the clay!
Bring two soles and carry one away.

Old Couplet

...you are obliged to cross the Moors they call the Black Hambledon over
which the road runs in narrow hollows that admit a south country chaise
with such difficulty that I reckon this part of the journey (was) made at the
hazard of my neck. The going down into Cleveland is beyond all descrip-
tion terrible...

Arthur Young (1771)

This ean nuight, this ean night,
Every night and awle:
Fire and Fleet and Candle-light,
And Christ receive thy Sawle.

Cleveland Lyke-Wake Dirge

Castle Howard

Nobody had informed me that I should at
once see a palace, a town, a fortified city,
temples in high places, woods worthy of
being each a metropolis of the Druids,
vales connected to other hills by other
woods, the noblest lawn in the world
fenced by half the horizon, and a mau-
soleum that would tempt one to be buried
alive.

Horace
Walpole

The Castle Howards and the Duncombes were the last word in residential
apparatus.

Ivor Brown (1932)

12

Coast

There is a nice - and almost a humorous - graduation about the Yorkshire sea-side resorts. Of the principal four, Bridlington is popular and Bank Holidayish; Whitby is grave, literary, artistic and aristocratic; Filey is just the place for honeymooning couples, old maids, and families; Scarborough is Filey, Whitby and Bridlington all rolled into one.

J. S. Fletcher (1908)

Saltburn is select and prettily placed; Filey, quiet, Bridlington bustling; and Redcar, safe...

M. J. B. Baddeley (1897)

Many lives are lost in these fisheries. It is a common saying at Staithes, "T'sea gat him", in speaking of a departed fisherman.

Thomas and Katharine MacQuoid (1894)

Mi missues knit this gansey (jersey) No, she didn't use a pattern. You can buy 'em, but you get halfway, and they're allus wrong.

Staithes fisherman (1981)

Port Mulgrave clings to Yorkshire with the tenacity of a limpet... Ironstone mines which provided its sole excuse for existence are long defunct. The harbour, deprived of a reason for survival... is being slowly tortured to death by the relentless North Sea waves.

David Joy (1966)

Runswick village huddles on the cliffside as though seeking shelter from the north wind that blows cruelly in winter. The foundations of the buildings cling tenuously to fickle clay that has been known to shake cottages into the sea like a careless hand casting dice.

Chris Scott Wilson (1982)

The thing I like most about Whitby,
I think it's incredible luck,
Is an ancient and moribund dredger
Dredging buckets and buckets of muck.

And when it has filled up its hopper
With a beautiful puddle of black
It takes it, and dumps it, outside of the harbour,
And the sea brings all of it back.

Pat Wilson (1966)

Red roofs bunched in a cleft hillside,
Salt-sprayed homesteads cling and hide,
Steeply, they climb from scar-torn seas,
In labyrinthine galleries.

Marjorie Atkinson at Robin Hoods Bay (1966)

Legend tells us that the Devil made Filey Brigg... He intended to continue it right across the North Sea, but tired of his labour. Geologists give a more prosaic explanation - that the upper beds of soft clay have been washed away, leaving only the solid substructure.

Local guide book

No wonder there has been sufficient sense among those who spend their lives in promoting schemes for ugly piers and senseless promenades to realise that Nature has supplied Filey with a more permanent and infinitely more attractive pier than their fatuous ingenuity could produce.

Gordon Home, Yorkshire (1908)

The sea cliff at Ravenscar is, in fact, two cliffs. It resembles a huge sofa set facing the sea. First there is an abrupt face, its food washed by the high tides and its rocks salt-encrusted by the winter gales, then a plateau - the seat of the sofa - backed by a further high cliff. According to the map, this is Beast Cliff and the name seems appropriate.

Malcolm Barker (1966)

14

July 3rd, 1769. Went to Flamborough Head... In some places the rocks are insulated, are of a pyramidal figure, and soar up to a vast height, the bases of most are solid, but in some pierced through, and arched. Multitudes of birds were swimming about, others swarmed in the air and almost stunned us with the variety of their croaks and screams.

Thomas Pennant, Tour to Scotland

For a thorough enjoyment of the east wind, commend us to Flamborough Head.

M. J. B. Baddeley, guidebook writer

We remained on deck all day lying on sofas. The sea was very rough towards evening and I was very ill. We reached Flamborough Head, on the Yorkshire coast, by half-past five.

Queen Victoria, on her first visit to Scotland (1842)

Bridlington Priory... stands out on the skyline as a beacon to the thousands of visitors to the town and is a welcoming sign to townsfolk returning from their travels.

Ernest Hutchinson (1980)

There is an ebbing and flowing well of fresh water in Bridlington harbour which flows when the level of the tide is within four feet of the shore, and continues until the tide has ebbed to the same level...

Bridlington guide

At Spurn, Yorkshire has its final impressive flourish. It sends out this finger of sand and gravel as though to tickle the ribs of Lincolnshire. The territorial advantage is precarious. What the tide has heaped up, another tide could so easily take away.

W. R. Mitchell (1966)

15

Crafts

Old Jamie's makkin' besoms,
An' Jackie's rivin' spells;
Dinah's fotchin' watter
Fra t'owd Spring Wells.

Dialect poem referring to the Ibbotsons of Threshfield

Craven

Amongst the mountains high
Of Craven,
Where blue heads for caps put on the sky.

Michael Drayton

Cricket

The joke about Yorkshire cricket is that for Yorkshiremen it is no laughing matter.

Neville Cardus

To those living outside the county, this abiding passion for cricket as a whole, and the Yorkshire side in particular, is something almost beyond comprehension.

Sydney Moorhouse (1967)

To Yorkshire cricketers, it has become rather more serious than a mere game. It is almost a religion.

Trevor Bailey, in Championship Cricket (1961)

Dale-country

O Swardill's good for horses,
An' Wensla-dill for cheese

And Airdill folk are busy as a bee;
But wheresoe're I wander,
My owd heart aye grows fonder
O'Whardill wheer I'll lig me doon an' dee.

F. W. Moorman

The farms are rich, well stocked and well attended to. The hay is said to be so nutritious that no other food is required to fatten the stock.

George Radford, about Wensleydale

One of the charms of the Yorkshire Dales is that they are all characteristically different, like lovely sisters of the same family.

Alfred J. Brown

An' way up-dale girt hills noo fold
Theer wings saw blue,
As guardian angels do, when work is done
An' neet is new.

Dorothy Una Ratcliffe

Dalesfolk

The dalesman is like many of the rivers among which he lives. He is slow but deep and, believe me, it takes years of constant touch with him before one can get into that happy position of being able to read him like a book.

"Wonten", Hawes (1939)

We shall never really understand the Pennine dalespeople until we realise their pre-occupation with sheep.

Ella Pontefract

No name has rung more resoundingly through Yorkshire history than that of Scrope. Three Scrope noblemen found their way into Shakespeare's historical plays. The influence of one of them, the eldest son of the first Lord

Scrope, was so vast that Shakespeare wrote of him "he hath the realm in farm."

Harry Mead (1982)

The Beresfords were always known for shooting, fishing and music.

Frank Beresford (1981)

I dreamt last night of England and the rain,
grey clouds across the Yorkshire hills, and mist
haunting the moors, curled low in every grain;
close-huddled sheep keeping bedraggled tryst
behind a broken wall; smell of wet heather;
music of rushing streams; beat of the wind;
one solitary shepherd... "Mucky weather!"...
"Aye, dampish...an' ah've three young lambs ti find."

William Cowley, during a sojourn in India

I began by buying half a waterfall with a small farm attached. Then I came to live at the farm and found that half a waterfall is absurd, so I bought the other half... Above me is the old packhorse highway that passes over Hell Gill bridge and connects Wensleydale with Brough... All my friends are poachers.

R. A. Scott Macfie (1920)

Don, river

In Sheffield, at t'Wicker, where t'water runs over t'weir, the river Don holds few charms for passers-by. But these grimy waters, life-blood of the city, rise in scenes of incomparable beauty to the north-west of the city.

Campion Barrows (1967)

Eskdale

...is the only Yorkshire valley of any size which has its ankles splashed by salt water... One moment there is a peaty-coloured stream rippling between dense foliage and the next there are mudbanks, boats and the incessant calling of gulls.

David Joy (1967)

Families

Almost every farm and cottage seems to be tenanted by a Mallaby - for the Mallabys are to Colsterdale what the Metcalfes are to Wensleydale, though there are not so many of them.

A. J. Brown (1939)

Farming

Oh, why don't these backroom bods
Firmly entrenched in their cushy jobs
Show us ignorant breeders how
To propagate a five-day cow.

Charles P. Wilson (1966)

Farndale

Like many another narrow valley gouged out of the moorland block of the North-East, it is a wait-and-see sort of place: deep-sunk, secluded.

W. R. Mitchell (1981)

Just why, or when, the daffodils came to Farndale is a matter for lively debate. The wild daffodil *(Narcissus pseudonarcissus)* is, of course, a native plant of Britain and grows in other locations in the North York Moors as well as in other parts of the British Isles.

National Park Information Service (1981)

Food

Here's tiv us, all on us, an' me an' all:
May we nivver want nowt, noan on us,
Ner me nawther.

The Yorkshire Toast

I sit down to venison, fish, and wild fowl, or a couple of fowls or ducks, with curds, strawberries and cream, and all the simple plenty which a rich valley can produce, with a clean cloth on my table, and a bottle of wine on my right hand to drink your health. Not a parishioner catches a hare, or a rabbit, or a trout, but he brings it as an offering to me. I am in high spirits.

Laurence Sterne, vicar of Coxwold, 1760-1768

See all, hear all, say nowt;
Eit all, sup all, pay nowt,
And if tha ivver does owt fer nowt
Do it for thissel.

A Yorkshire Commandment

The hospitality for which they are famous gave rise to the term "Yorkshire Bite".

William Andrews, Picturesque Yorkshire.

We have had for breakfast toast, cakes, a Yorkshire pie, a piece of beef about the size and much the shape of my portmanteau, tea, coffee, ham and eggs.

Charles Dickens, in a letter to his wife (1838)

What a feast we had! Strong tea and abundance of sugar and rich cream. We laid the delicious butter on our bread in such thick clumps... There was brown-bread toast too, and fried ham and eggs, and more honey, and Yorkshire cake.

Juliana Horatia Ewing

Weighing 1 1/2lb, a Barnsley chop is something to be remembered. It is cut from the loins of a sheep, and in some cases it is not possible to get more than two chops from a sheep.

H.D.

Belly keeps t'back up; you can't work without some packing.

Big Bill, Swaledale

I have found the richness of Yorkshire food a little overpowering. Cream, butter, eggs, flour and all the other enemies of the dietician are in full use here. "What do you think of Yorkshire pudding?" I am frequently asked. Well, I've eaten this half a dozen times, and it has been a different shape, size and colour each time. I've had it with, without, under and above gravy, with and without meat. I am extremely confused. The whole thing is too mysterious.

Allan Eady, a visiting American (1966)

Gliding

Fifty years ago, Yorkshire gained an airborne attraction that has remained popular ever since. Organised gliding took wing at Sutton Bank. Today, the sight of gliders soaring high above the bank is so familiar that few give a thought as to how gliding became established, which was not long after the introduction of gliding into Britain in 1922.

Harry Mead (1983)

Goathland

> Wee'r Gooadlon' pleeaf stots cum'd agean
> All dek't wi' ribbons foair,
> Seea noo we'll dea the best we can
> An' the best can dea na mair.

Goathland Plough Stots song

The Plough Stots are a team of sword-dancers who dance up and down the long village streets, hauling a plough and begging for alms. In olden days, there were said to "shake the mud off their clogs and make merry." Only when they were refused did they plough a furrow through the offender's front lawn.

*H. J.
S. (1980)*

Greenhow Hill

Well! It's as near heaven as ever you'll get.

*Farmer, to Rev J. M.
Chadwick, the new vicar*

It was on a March morning when I saw (from Greenhow) the reflection of the rising sun, like a streak of blood on the surface of the North Sea, a matter of about 80 miles away.

Harald Bruff

The Miner's Arms, Greenhow's local, plainly epitomises the story of the village. Today the public is "as thrang iv a Saturday neet" as it was in the heyday of the Hill's mining activity.

Dorothy Ashman (1972)

Harrogate

...the queerest place, with the strangest people in it, leading the oddest lives.

Charles Dickens, commenting on the Spa activity (1853)

Those who have seen the film "Agatha" will know that the spa was a going concern as recently as 1926, the year when the missing Agatha Christie took refuge in the *Old Swan*. On a single morning in that year, 1,500 glasses of sulphur water were served in the Royal Pump Room.

Arnold Kellett (1981)

Hawes

Hawes has a linear appearance, between fell and riverside flats. Half a dozen good roads converge upon the town. Hawes is a cultural centre, a staging post for visitors, a town abounding with shops and services of benefit to dalesfolk and to tourists.

W. R. M. (1983)

Hebden Bridge

Every so often, when I was a child, we'd go to visit relatives in Hebden Bridge. I remember the first journey especially because I'd never heard of the place, and I had no idea where it was. Hebden bridge was just another name to add to my uncle's succession of homes in the foreign countries of

23

Heckmondwike and Cleckheaton.

Michael North (1983)

The town has that indefinable quality called "character".

T. S.

Horse

A true northcountry breed is the Cleveland Bay, developed as a carriage horse and still carrying out that function on the most magnificent of State occasions.

Edward Hart (1967)

Huddersfield

I rode over the mountains to Huddersfield. A wilder people I never saw in England. The men, women and children filled the streets and seemed just ready to devour us.

John Wesley (1757)

Huddersfield - hills, mills, music. To hear *The Messiah* performed by the Choral Society is pure delight. To wear a suit made from fine Huddersfield worsted is the height of sartorial elegance.

Hazel Wheeler (1982)

I'd never seen anything like the big, black stone buildings of Huddersfield. Especially the e-n-o-r-m-o-u-s town hall. Many of the buildings seemed colossal.

Thelma Barlow, recalling a move from a small village (1993)

They were good people, warm-hearted, with a kind of shyness about them - and such gratitude.

A Doctor in the 1950s

...this happy, friendly, open town.

S. L. Henderson Smith

Hull and Humber

Hull is... clean as the best parts of London and the people as bustling and attentive.

William Cobbett

Hull had the honour of possessing the first enclosed trading dock in Great Britain (1778) It proved to be a great success...

H. B. Browne

> Oft-times I've sat and watched the tide
> Where Wolds of Yorks and Lincs divide,
> Down on the peaceful Humberside...

M. T. Sonley (1967)

Curiosity has led to an expert estimating that one-and-a-quarter million tons of silt are always in suspension in the River Humber.

Charles Dixon

Humber...a common rendezvous for the greatest part of the rivers hereabouts.

Camden, Elizabethan topographer

Hull, a frightful, dirty, brickhousey, tradesmanlike, rich, vulgar place; yet the river - though the shores are so low that they can hardly be seen - looked beautiful with the lights upon it, and boats moving about.

Dorothy Wordsworth, The Grasmere Journal (1802)

Through all its changes, the Humber remains the pulsing artery of Yorkshire without which the county would languish.

Harry J. Scott

No ship is worked so consistently, hard and long, or does such a variety of work, as the salt-stained tug-boat, over 60 of which cover the Humber ports.

A. T. (1960)

The Humber Bridge is proving to be quite an attraction... It is certainly an impressive structure, seen at its aesthetic best from the Lincolnshire approach road, thought most visitors start their exploring from the northern end.

Captain D. C. Thomas (1983)

Hunmanby

One of the most populous villages in North Yorkshire, Hunmanby nestles in the lee of a wooded escarpment on the edge of the Wolds.

Simon Dore (1983)

...a little town.

John Wesley (1784)

Ilkley

As we passed Burley, the glaring white house of Ilkley Fountain, stuck as it were midway on the steep ascent of the Rumbold-moor, beckoned our immediate approach to the Spa village. We halted at the *New Inn*, a stone building, the last in this primitive and simple village, going towards Skipton...

A. B. Granville (1841)

With its excellent bus and rail links to Leeds and Bradford, Ilkley has become commuter-land, but far from making it into a social wasteland, the influx of teachers, TV producers and a variety of executives has helped to strengthen its identity as a town.

John Hewitt (1982)

Ingleborough

A mountain so cruel, yet so kind, which I still love to climb, can have only one name - Ingleborough.

Anne Walker (1972)

This hill spans such a vast area it is not surprising to find such variation in the routes to and from the summit. My favourite approach has always been that superb nature trail leading from Clapham through Clapdale Wood and by Ingleborough Cave to Trow Gill and the open moor beyond.

Kenneth Oldham (1983)

Knaresborough

Wherever you wander, in and out of Knaresborough's ways and byways, some old tale is lying in wait.

Halliwell Sutcliffe

What really takes your breath away - certainly if this is your first visit - is when you stroll from the Market Place into the Castle grounds and then stand and gaze down at the fairy-tale gorge, which makes the setting of Knaresborough unique.

Arnold Kellett (1983)

Leeds

Of busy Leeds, upwafting to the clouds
The incense of thanksgiving; all is joy,
And trade and business guide the living scene.

John Dyer (1757)

The words "Lucky Leeds" are seldom used nowadays. The clothing capital was certainly lucky as regards bombing during the 1939-45 war, considering its importance in the industrial war effort. The enduring luck of Leeds is its situation, on the edge of despoilation... and adjacent to some of the finest country in Yorkshire.

J. B. (1982)

Limestone

Going up this deep limestone fissure (Trollers Gill, near Appletreewick) you note the absence of water and the presence of boulders of various shapes and sizes... The foot of the rocks has been washed so much that the tops considerably over-hang... and you soon find yourself shut in by lofty hills.

John Crowther (1858-1930)

At last, at the bottom of a hill they came to a spring, a real North Country limestone fountain, like one of those in Sicily, or Greece.

Charles Kingsley at Malham Cove

People with marked suicidal tendencies have been known to attempt difficult climbs on limestone crags. This of course is sheer folly as limestone simply cannot be trusted not to break off or come away in large clumps upon the slightest provocation.

Godfrey Wilson (1939)

Castleberg rock stands high above the town (Settle) and seems almost human in its changing ways and temperament. On a summer day, it is full bright with the off-yellow of the sun which in the glint of the evening turns to a deep mellow orange. And as the sun lulls its head under a hazy hill, so too the rock seems to blow out its candle of colours for the night and sit there and meditate.

J. R. Burns (1966)

Malton

You will not go thirsty in Malton's closely-grouped selection of public houses. Worth a visit for a look at its Norman stone-vaulted crypt is the *Cross Keys Inn* in Wheelgate. The crypt was a rest house belonging to the Old Malton Priory in medieval times and now forms part of the pub's cellar.

Simon Dore (1983)

Middleham

Situated between East and West Witton, and thus logically named, is Middleham: perched proudly upon a hill between the rivers Cover and Ure... In its heyday, the castle, with the largest keep in England, must have looked magnificent and was referred to as the Windsor of the North.

Sonia Lawson (1993)

Mills

It was a northern city, a forest of grey stone. Mills, like fortresses, loomed enormously.

Walter Wilkinson

At hauf past five Tha leaves thi bed,
An off Tha goes to wark;
An gropes thi way to Mill or Shed,
Six months o' th year ith dark.
Tha gets but little for Thi pains,
But that's noa fault o' Thine,
Thi Master reckons up his gains,
And ligs i' bed till nine.

John Hartley

Bradford is a great emporium of the woollen trade, and the first impression created in the mind of the stranger is that it consists almost entirely of mills.

M. J. B. Baddeley (1897)

Mining, coal

Featherstone was one of the dirtiest mining villages in the North of England. The dust blew on everybody. The wealthy proportion of the community - which was very small - also had dust in their homes. I later wrote a novel which opened with this classless distribution of dust from the slagheaps.

John Finch (1982)

Mining, lead

The mines at Grassington sent their lead and silver from the smelt mills to Gargrave and Leeds by pack-horse train, bringing back coal and stores, while at an earlier period, mines from all over the Dales area sent their lead to the great lead markets of Kirkby Malzeard or Yarm. The roads made by this traffic can still be traced over most of the remoter moorlands of the dales.

Arthur Raistrick (1941)

Moors

A heaven so clear, an earth so calm,
So sweet, so soft, so hushed an air,

And deepening still the dream-like charm
Wild moor-sheep feeding everywhere.

Emily Bronte at Haworth

The moors around (Malhamdale) are truly wild and romantic. Nature sits in solitary grandeur... It would be highly imprudent for a stranger to travel these moors without a guide, as he would risk the danger of perishing for want; or the probable chance of breaking his neck down some precipice in the dark, or from being caught in a fog.

Edward Dayes (1763-1804)

They're leadin' brekkons doon fra' moors
For cattle-beddin'
On track 'at goes by t'larch plantation
To opur Tom steadin'.

Dorothy Una Ratcliffe

If you have travelled on foot from Hawes to Ingleton, you are a walker; and if you have braved the autumn winds tearing over those moorland miles, you are also a wrestler.

Lois Victor Coppin

Given up, stone back to stone,
The house alone,
Abandoned, till the moor
Takes back its own.

C. Brandon (1978)

Gamekeepers and shepherds are the twin agencies who have preserved the heather as we know it. Their weapon is the match, applied to a tuft of dead grass or bracken in late winter, and the resulting flame buried into the heart of a heather bed.

Edward Hart (1982)

The moors play their part in shaping character, and the Yorkshire moorland folk are sturdy and independent, but as one elderly man pointed out: "We aren't Heathcliffs or Old Josephs by any means, though some people expect us to be."

Marion Troughton

The scenery in these western moors is often wild and weird.

Bulmer's Directory (1890)

Reverently, I add my footsteps to those of pannierman, farmer, forester, man-at-arms, esquire, knight, baron, the medieval iron-workers and all the motley throng, less enduring than the stones on which they rudely tramp.

Frank Elgee (d.1944) about the North York Moors

Morality

There are things they do at Buckden;
At Arncliffe, and Aptrick, too,
That we, who live in Burnsall,
Would rather die than do,
With Grassington's behaviour,
We don't see eye to eye;
For the moral tone of Burnsall
Is very, very high.

A Yorkshire Tyke (1941)

Nonconformity

A religion of Hell-fire and brimstone once burnt fiercely in the valley, forging a few individuals into latter-day Moses'. In the 1760s, a former collier-turned-dynamic evangelist called Dan Taylor quarried stone from the moors above Hebden and carted it off on his own back to build a meeting-house, as if to bring back the Word carved on Millstone Grit.

Michael North (1983)

Pateley Bridge

You can travel to the edge of the earth and I'll gamble you'll come across someone who at sometime has either lived in or has relations or friends hailing from one or other of these prolific hives of industry, the yards of Pateley Bridge.

W. A. Johnson

Pennines

I was always very proud of living in the West Riding of Yorkshire, in that hilly part which is called the backbone of England, the Pennine Chain... At night I loved to see the lighted trams climbing up the dark hills like fireflies on black velvet; it seemed to me that they were brave and sturdy, like Yorkshire people, not afraid of difficult tasks or big hills.

Phyllis Bentley, novelist, in a newspaper interview

The Pennine Way...Great North Roof.

Ivor Brown

The first time I travelled the road to Cosh - if road it could be named - was in mid-winter snow. Soon after leaving Foxup, the drifts lay piled to the wall-tops. Only a narrow space of track was cleared, winding endlessly, it seemed, into a wilderness above. No bird called. The wind was silent. All the land stretched damp and empty to a leaden sky. Then a farm-dog barked noisily, and the relief was instant. Something was alive, after all, in this land that seemed to have lain dead for unnumbered ages.

Halliwell Sutcliffe

33

There is nothing very picturesque about Cam (near the source of the Wharfe). Two rough, grim stone houses and a few pastures bitten into the moor give it an altogether austere appearance, even in summer.

A. J. Brown

Pickering

The town lies on the northern bank of a prehistoric lake. Now the lake has dried out into a fertile vale, 20 miles long and some five to ten miles wide.

Jean Raine (1982)

Poverty

> Dahn at heels, aht at toes,
> Aht o' work, an i' owd close,
> Short o' brass, friends few,
> then its winter.

From an old Yorkshire newspaper

Railway (Settle-Carlisle)

I started to explore the country north of Skipton and discovered the rural charms of places like Bell Busk; the rugged splendours and impressive loneliness of Ribblesdale with its three peaks, its potholes and rushing waters; the placid beauty of Dentdale; the magnificence of Wild Boar Fell dominating Ais Gill and the kindness of the Eden Valley. And through it all there ran the most marvellous railway which seemed as much at home as the rocks and the rivers.

Eric Treacy, in a foreword to Rails in the Fells (1973)

The railway is distinguished by its straightness. It meant to get to Scotland in the fastest possible time and would brook no delays. If a hill got in the way, the Settle-Carlisle went straight through it - either by tunnel or cutting... Its viaducts are titanic examples of Victorian architecture, built by men who clearly believed that while the impossible might take a little longer, it had better not take too long.

Yorkshire Life (1976)

Ribblehead Viaduct, absolutely alone in a wilderness of rough windblown moorland, with 2,414ft Whernside as a backcloth, is one of the most dramatically situated engineering works in England.

Peter E. Baughan, Centenary of the Long Drag (1976)

Richmond

...a magic place of tall towers, that of the Grey Friars being one of the most graceful in England; of narrow alleyways called "wynds", just as in Edinburgh; of ancient postern-gates, a cobbled market-place on a slope, and to crown all a tremendous square Norman castle standing on an unscalable rock above the cascading, winding Swale.

S. P. B. Mais

The people of Richmond need no time-telescope to bring history into focus. The past is ever present.

Fred Hurrell (1983)

Ripley

Any man who has money can build a house, but few can show the same house his family has lived in so many years as the Ingilbys have done at Ripley.

Sir John Ingilby (1780)

This place is much in demand by television companies who are anxious to evoke the rural past. "The television aerials in the village tend to go up and down on elastic... We have so many layers of paint on the castle windows that we can barely open any of them," says Sir Thomas Ingilby.

W. R. Mitchell (1983)

Ripon

When I entered Ripon, the market place was crowded with cattle and holiday folk... After parading the fair and staring at the booth, the misses and the Scotch cattle, I sat down to a good dinner, trout and roast fowl...

Lord Torrington (1780)

To see Ripon at its best you need to get up early on a sparkling summer morning, when birdsong is heard in the streets and the fresh air blowing down from the moors has not been swamped by traffic fumes. Or perhaps in a summer day, when folk stroll in the square and the Americans follow the Wakeman as he sounds the curfew... Ripon stands at the meeting of three rivers, with its interests still firmly based on the land.

Ann Williams

Rivers

Castleford lasses may weel be fair,
For they wesh i' t'Calder, and sind i' t'Aire.

Anon

Wharfe is clear, and Aire is lythe,
Where the Aire drowns one, Wharfe drowns five.

Anon

Where Tees, full many a fathom low,
Wears with his rage no common foe;
Nor pebbly bank, nor sand bed here,
Nor clay mount checks his fierce career;
Condemn'd to mine a channel'd way
O'er solid sheets of marble grey.

Walter Scott, at Rokeby (1812)

36

Roads

In the Dales, it's a constant switchback ride with frequent suprises from sheep and cows and buses and milk vans and fearful notices which warn the driver of dangerous hills. I shall have to walk down the hill into Dent some-day. I have done it by car, but I wasted all my effort in nervous exhaustion by clinging to the hillside in desperation. It all goes down - to experience.

Allan Eady, a visiting American (1966)

Roseberry Topping

...it's the biggest hill i' all Yorksheer... a mahle an' a haufe heegh, an' as cawd as ice at t'top on't, i' t'yattest day i' summer.

From a local play, "Margery Moorpout"

Roseberry Topping, though only 1,022 feet in height, is by reason of its con-ical shape and its isolated position as an outpost of the dull level-topped range... far the most striking of the eminences of the Cleveland district.

M. J. B. Baddeley (1897)

Rosedale

It is a deeply-dissected dale and would be called a combe in Devon and a cwn in Wales.

John Hillaby (1982)

I walked down t'Bank (one in two and a-half) and suddenly found I was looking straight into me wellies.

Rosedale Resident

Seasons

If it would only get dry and warm enough to sit out, I could get some work done. But winter is uncertain always. A storm starts and finishes, but drizzle seems to go on for ever...

...It's nice to see a bit of real spring with blue sky among the clouds.

Fred Lawson, Dales artist (1966)

The Hornsea spring is not marked by the first cuckoo but by the coming of the first tourists - by the first chatter from the caravan sites, the first car-park full signs near the seafront, and by the first triumphal shouts of "bingo".

W. R. Mitchell (1966)

Autumn, or "back end", as we say in these parts, used to be associated with the end of the harvest, the first threshing days and ploughing the stubbles. Now, the Spring barley must be sown and on many High Wold farms it's all hustle and bustle to get the "taties" in.

Irene Megginson (1982)

Sheep

Sheep don't get fat up here.

Bob Middleton, at Cam Houses (1980)

I know a lot of useless things, of course, but I can't tell one sheep from another; so the dalesfolk are rather sorry for me and try to put me at my ease - which, after all, is just good manners.

R. A. Scott Macfie (1922)

My boss would stand and watch and smoke his pipe, and say of one animal: "She'll lamb afore mornin". And she did. He really watched his sheep.

North Ribblesdale farmer

Clipping day was a grand day, and everybody had a good laugh. Owd-fashioned jokes were flying around. Women made sandwiches, and the farmer's wife made a big tatie pie. Tea was served in big cans.

Swaledale recollection

Shipley

Oh Shipley Glen, Oh Shipley Glen,
To Bradford hearts so dear;
The seaside is so far away
But the Salt-aire is always here.

Traditional Rhyme

Speyks

Swat-tha-doon. (Sit you down, Swaledale)

It's ossin' ta slaat. (Trying to rain, Huddersfield)

If he had a maathful o' gumboils, he couldn't thoil to part wi' one. (West Yorkshire)

He's ovver tiered to goa to sleep. (Of a dull Methodist preacher, Richmond)

Yon chap's that stuck up, ah reckon he'd be 'ard pressed to talk to hisself!

Well, it wean't rain up, will it?

Nivver buy owt wi' a wooden handle; it allus means hard work!

Wedded life is like a collop o' home-fed bacon, a strawk o' fat an' a strawk o' lean.

Ther's noa doctor's fissick can equal a hearty laff an' a contented mind.

It's a hard job to find onnybody at'll admit they've had enuff of owt they like.

It were all right till I had it mended.

Stately Homes

Castle Howard has the qualities of gusto and exuberant surprise. It is not a serene house, but one full of life and vigour. The stone changes colour according to the weather and the light changes the texture enormously. It has a sculptural quality. Inside, it is friendly and ungloomy.

George Howard, the owner (1966)

Swaledale

It is a twisty dale, unlike most of the other large dales which have long, straight sections. As you go up Swaledale, every view is different.

Lawrence Barker (1967)

Beautiful Swaledale, the land of rest,
Beautiful Swaledale, I love thee the best.
The land is set in a cultivate style;
The extension of Swaledale is twenty long mile.

Yorkshire Ballad

To see them all (Swaledale waterfalls) in flood with their white tails gallop-
ing down the mist-screened hills and craggy steeps, and the amber-foamed
cataracts leaping madly in the valley below, is to witness a scene truly
Alpine in its wild and forbidding grandeur.

Harry Speight (1897)

It is interesting to find that when local folk go down to Richmond, they
regard it as a journey outside the dale. To them, Swaledale proper ends just
after Grinton.

David Joy (1967)

Teesdale

This dale has a unique vernacular architecture of white-washed farmhouses,
cottages, barns and groups of farm buildings. They date from the mid-18th
century onwards and, co-inciding with the Great Enclosure of 1761 to 1844,
are in an architectural idiom which is Mediterranean in appearance. In con-
sequence, they are an unexpected and dramatic intrusion into the northern
countryside.

F. W. Bickerton (1980)

Teesmouth

Before the vast and odorous industrial complex had spread itself like a
growth over the great estuary, the marshy wastes of the Teesmouth were
measured in square miles rather than in acres. They formed one of the most
extensive wetlands of the British Isles. Even today, when the immense tract
has been reduced by reclamation, it remains a place of enrichment for the
naturalist.

Frederick Watson (1981)

Thornton-le-Dale

By common consent, this is recognised as one of the prettiest villages in
Yorkshire - not just in the official guide book but by virtually everyone who
has written his impressions of the place over the years.

Simon Dore (1983)

Towns

Helmsley is still strongly reminiscent of an estate village, and indeed much of it is owned by the Duncombe Park Estate, which controls about 24,000 acres. Since coaching days, it has been a popular stopping point for travellers and holidaymakers journeying from the West and North Ridings to the east coast.

David Joy (1967)

We've had our excitement at Howden. They built the R.100 airship here. When it was scrapped, we settled down to a quiet life again.

A Resident of Howden (1966)

In a part of Yorkshire where red bricks are numbered in trillions, you find that Pontefract has a pleasant profusion of grey stones. In a district where small villages suddenly rocketed into populous towns with the onset of industrialisation, Pontefract has kept its sense of history.

W. R. Mitchell (1966)

Trees

The most familiar tree on the barer limestone uplands of Yorkshire is the stunted hawthorn, gnome-like in the fantastic attitudes adopted by its trunk and branches.

Arthur Raistrick (1945)

Visitors

May 14th, 1800. Wm. and John (Wordsworth) set of into Yorkshire after dinner at half-past two o' clock, cold pork in their pockets.

Dorothy Wordsworth. The Grasmere Journal. (William married Sarah Hutchinson, who lived near Scarborough)

Walden

An eerie dale, with a few farms and few inhabitants.

Edmund Bogg, Victorian guidebook writer

If there's snow on the north-east wind, it will fall on Walden...Even in a decent winter, we are blocked in.

Walden farmer

Weather

I find it difficult to prepare for the constant changes in the weather (in the Dales) You wake to a brilliant morning, spend the afternoon sheltering from the tropical downpour and in the evening admire the splendour of the sunset. In New York, you can be 90% sure of the day and dress accordingly.

Allan Eady, a New Yorker in the Dales (1966)

When Roseberry Topping wears a cap
Let Cleveland then beware a clap.

Traditional

Wind? They should have a notice in these parts: "Beware of low-flying sheep".

Heard at Tan Hill Inn

I toured (the Pennines) on foot in wind, slush and sleet, for the benefit of my heart.

R. A. Scott Macfie (1917)

Wolds

I want to go back to Yorkshire and the Wolds, and the smell of tarred ropes and wool, and horses in the dark barns there, and the granaries full of sliding gold and smelling of dust, the sloping field, and slow-speaking shrewd workers.

Winifred Holtby

We had an interesting ride over the Wolds, though it rained all the way. Single thorn bushes were scattered about on the turf, sheep sheds here and there, and now and then a little hut. Swelling grounds and sometimes a single tree or clump of trees.. .

Dorothy Wordsworth, The Grasmere Journal (1802)

Work

Hard wark's killed neabody, but thowt's on it's killed mony a thoosand.

Peat-cutter, Eskdale

York

Yorke, Yorke, for my monie,
Of all the cities that ever I see,
For merry pastime and companie.

Old Ballad

Yorkshireness

Yorkshire presents within itself perhaps the most complete epitome of physical geography and geological study to be found in any other equal area on the globe.

M. Tait

Yorkshire folk seem to be the most individual and diverse I have yet met. Sometimes it is a little nerve-racking to face their positive and, if I may be forgiven, almost blunt approach; but at the end of an interview you are left in little doubt of their opinion. This is encouraging when you think you have made a good impression and discouraging when you known you haven't.

Allan Eady, a visiting American (1966)

The North is a fat and generous sow lying on her side while the greedy little pigs (the South) feed off her.

Graham Turner, quoting a Batley man (1967)

I still think of Yorkshire as home. And every autumn the same nostalgic feeling comes over me - I am homesick for the sight of purple heather on the moors.

Naomi Jacob, novelist

Hen oils, clogs an' home-fed bacon;
dry bread, cricket wi' corky balls;
summer suns an' speckled birds' eggs;
chips - wi' bits on; cuckoo calls...

Parkin, bullseyes, thick spanish juice;
savvery ducks wi' a sting o' spice;
rowly poly puddins tumblin'
aht o' t'cloth all jammy and nice.

Traditional

Market research indicates a low consumption of milk and cheese despite the Yorkshireman's love of apple pie with cheese and his delight in milk puddings. Strong tea is preferred and it must mash long enough, usually in a metal teapot.

Bryan Waites (1983)

Illustrations

THE NORTH'S LEADING PUBLISHER
FOR MORE THAN 40 YEARS

Here is a selection of other books that may interest you:

YORKSHIRE'S YAMMER
(ISBN 1 85568 077 7)
THE GREAT YORKSHIRE JOKE BOOK
(ISBN 1 85568 081 5)
FAVOURITE YORKSHIRE HUMOUR
(ISBN 1 85568 048 3)
BEST YORKSHIRE TALES
(ISBN 1 85568 030 0)
TEACH THISSEN TYKE
(ISBN 1 85206 921 9)
TALES FROM THE DALESMAN
(ISBN 1 85568 068 8)
YORKSHIRE WIT AND WISDOM
(ISBN 1 85568 011 4)

With over 150 books to choose from the Dalesman range covers
subjects as diverse as:
WALKING, WILDLIFE, HUMOUR, TOPOGRAPHY, ANTHOLO-
GIES, HOLIDAY GUIDES, GHOSTS AND SPORT

For a catalogue of all the Dalesman titles send a SAE to:
DALESMAN PUBLISHING CO LTD
CLAPHAM, VIA LANCASTER, LA2 8EB